SKY TRUCK 2

SKY TRUCK 2

Stephen Piercey

Osprey Colour Series

Published in 1986 by Osprey Publishing Limited
27A Floral Street, London WC2E 9DP
Member company of the George Philip Group

British Library Cataloguing in Publication Data

Piercey, Stephen
    Sky truck 2.—(Osprey colour series)
    1. Transport planes—History—Pictorial works
    I. Title
    629.133′340423   TL685.4

ISBN 0-85045-704-1

Editor Dennis Baldry
Designed by Norman Brownsword
Printed in Hong Kong

Introduction

Anyone who already has a copy of *SKY TRUCK* on their bookshelf will not need to be told that *SKY TRUCK 2* is devoted to the classic piston-engined airliners of yesteryear. If you're new to the world of the big recips, welcome aboard. Sit back, stuff some cotton wool in your ears and pop a barley sugar in your mouth, because for the next 120 pages soporific high-tech jetliners, with their colour-CRT displays and other gismo-goodies, are *out*. Gas-guzzling old clunks rule, OK?

It may not be common knowledge that Stephen Piercey was tragically killed in a flying accident on 20 May 1984, shortly before *SKY TRUCK* was published. This sequel would not have been possible without the consent, patience, and encouragement of Ray and Patsy Piercey, Stephen's parents. I would also like to thank them for their hospitality during the hours I spent sifting through his vast collection of transparencies. About 90 per cent of the material I've selected was shot after *SKY TRUCK* went to press in November 1983.

Happily, *Propliner*, the magazine which Stephen Piercey founded and edited to cater for piston-engined and turboprop transport aircraft enthusiasts, is now back on the streets. Former assistant editor Tony Merton Jones is now in the left-hand seat.

There is, of course, a missing dimension to the captions. Steve's unique knowledge of the propliner population died with him. I've given it my best shot, and I apologize for any errors or omissions.

Like *SKY TRUCK*, the photographs in this book were all taken with Nikon cameras and lenses, loaded with Kodachrome 25 and 64.

Dennis Baldry
Osprey Publishing Limited
London, January 1986

Front cover Most Western airlines were equipped with the Douglas DC-6 before the big jets relegated the type to low-cost charter and cargo work. The DC-6B (pictured) is powered by four 2500 hp Pratt & Whitney R-2800-CB17 radials, giving a cruising speed of 316 mph. About 60 examples of the 'Six' remain active, surviving on ad hoc cargo business in South America and Africa

Back cover Rurrenabaque, Bolivia, as seen from the forward door of a Frigorificos Reyes' DC-4

Title pages The editor's photograph of a very special Vickers Viscount, taken at Southend Airport on 28 January 1986. Thanks to Mike Kay, the commercial director of British Air Ferries, G-APIM was officially named *Viscount Stephen Piercey* on 25 August 1984 during a ceremony attended by the Piercey family and many of Stephen's friends. Before she was purchased by BAF, G-APIM saw extensive service with British European Airways and British Airways; during his career with BEA one Ray Piercey captained 'India Mike' on numerous occasions

Back in 1977, Stephen Piercey made one of his many trips to South American and he couldn't resist posing in this remarkable Boeing B-17 Flying Fortress, operated as a meat wagon out of La Paz, Bolivia, by Frigorificos Reyes. CP-891 bears evidence of a neat wartime battle-damage repair below the flight-deck window

Contents

Bolivian odyssey

In the rarified 13,000 ft-high atmosphere of La Paz, Bolivia, you really do have to trust in God and Pratt & Whitney if you're flying a Curtiss C-46 Commando. With 2000 hp of tired iron turning on either side, CP-974 *Super Raton* ('Super Mouse') is held against the brakes while the pilot checks for any tell-tale mag drop. The single-engined performance of a C-46 is less than sparkling—you don't climb, you don't maintain height, you just head earthwards

Synchronicity: *Super Raton's* R-2800-34s ping into
life and start to hit that perfect beat. You can
almost hear it . . .

Resplendent in its polished, natural metal finish, the broad-shouldered Commando bounds across a rudimentary taxiway. When this picture was taken in April 1984, CP-974 was operated by meat-hauler Empresa Transportes Aereos Ltda. The aircraft is festooned with a variety of aerials for direction finding and communications

Overleaf A local Indian woman looks on as *Super Raton* rumbles past

Kicking up some dust, CP-974 taxies out for takeoff

Retractable tailwheel locked and main gears
chocked, *Super Raton* takes a break between
operations. Maintenance is carried out in the open
as a matter of routine—hangarage is a luxury most
Bolivian operators cannot afford or don't need,
probably both. Rudderless DC-3 CP-607 in
background is owned by Transportes Aereos
Tadeo (TAT)

Framed by a snow-sprinkled peak rising from the
altiplano, a C-46 stands with its cargo door held
open

Right Empresa Transportes Aereos Ltda is one of
about a dozen meat-haulers which operate out of
La Paz. Another of their faithful Commandos,
CP-1593, comes home after foraging in the
Bolivian hinterland

The Commando is a big airplane, a dominating 21 ft 8 in tall, 78 ft 4 in long, and with a wing span of exactly 108 ft. It must have seemed huge when the civil CW-20 first flew in March 1940. The demands of war left no room for the manufacture of commercial models; 3141 examples of the military C-46 were completed when production ceased in 1945

Right After a disasterous start the C-46 became a hero of the Hump, the China airlift over the Himalayas from Burma and India in WW2. Old-timers who flew the C-46 along the route back in 1943–45 will probably appreciate the airmanship of this Commando crew as they gain altitude to clear the Andes. Also pictured on the following page, CP-1593 was photographed from the flight-deck of another Commando, CP-754

The equipment might be old, but its paid for and
a good deal more practical than alternative forms
of Bolivian transportation. Road and rail
development is hamstrung by national poverty and
awesome natural obstacles

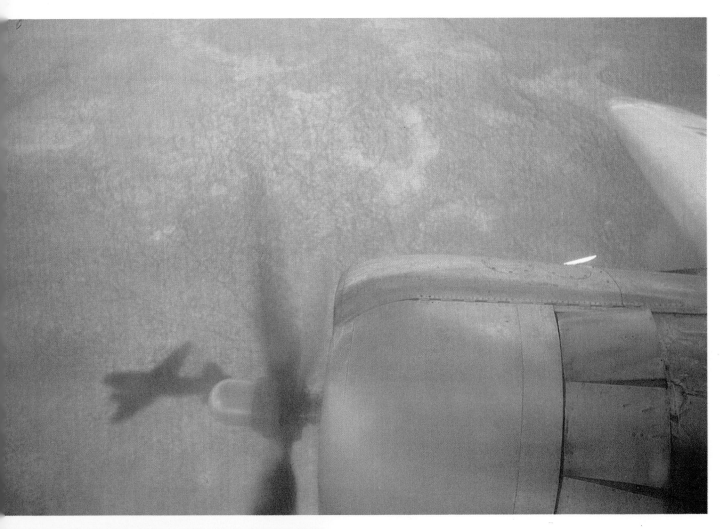

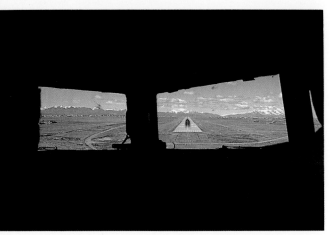

Commando CP-754 chases its own shadow across the landscape. **Left** Past the outer marker: a DC-6 on finals for La Paz Airport. **Overleaf** An ex-*Luftwaffe* F-4 front-seater is the chief pilot of Eldorado Ltda, an outfit which consists solely of this C-46 Commando, CP-1617

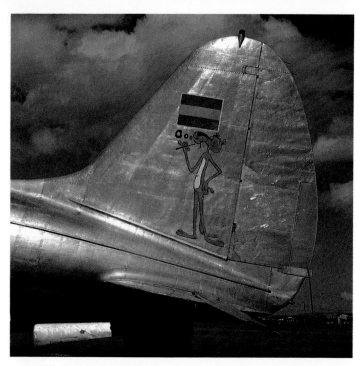

Downtime for CP-1244, another member of the Empresa Transportes Aereos Ltda fleet. The Pink Panther seems to be impersonating Noel Coward

This page and overleaf In April 1984, Transportes Aereos Universal Ltda operated two Commandos, but CP-1588 was subsequently written off after an accident. Large chunks of the aircraft were still cloistered around Universal's premises at La Paz in May 1985. Bolivia suffers from a high rate of illiteracy, so the motif on the fin may have a serious purpose

Frigorifico Santa Rita operate two Commandos,
CP-754 (pictured) and CP-1848. A lone DC-3
(CP-529) is also in its inventory

Well worn, CP-754 exudes rugged dependability. The wide track landing gear and generous flap area are vital for short-field survival

Taxying out for takeoff at La Paz, CP-754 is
bound for a remote farm in the Bolivian lowlands

Line-up and hold. Before he pushes the throttles
forward for takeoff, the pilot will let the airplane
run forward to straighten the tailwheel

Down on the farm, a specially adapted ox-cart is used to reach the cargo door. Bolivia is not a major beef producer like Brazil or Argentina—most of its livestock consists of sheep and goats. **Right** A safer, more substantial walkway was employed for the second batch of slaughtered animals

Universal's surviving C-46, CP-1655, tops up with oil and gasoline at Espiritu

CP-1655 looked rather lack-lustre back in April 1984. The old Commando has since been resprayed in a smart white/off-white/azure blue livery, highlighted by black engines and nacelles

Above Think pink: this intriguing Pink Panther character adorns the tail of DC-6 CP-1654

Let me fly again . . . this Frigorificos Reyes' Douglas DC-4, CP-1517, looks like a candidate for canibalization or the nearest dump, but a transfusion of spare parts and a coat (or two) of paint may produce a Phoenix-like transformation

Ready to roll. A Frigorificos Reyes' DC-4, CP-1653, waits for takeoff clearance at La Paz before departing for Rurrenabaque, 160 miles to the north along the river Beni

Right The same airplane at Rurrenabaque after an uneventful landing on the grass field

DC-4 CP-1653 off-loading supplies

DC-6 CP-1650 after disgorging a respectable tally
of fuel drums

Above and right Rolling. Every inch of the grass strip is used in the quest for airspeed. If the aircraft unsticks a little late, the pilot of this DC-6 may have to contend with a load of timber he hadn't bargained for. But no sweat: the big Pratts are pulling strongly, the field is hard, the grass nice and short. Add 20 degrees of flap and you've got it made

Overleaf Frigorificos Reyes' DC-4 CP-1207 sits it out at La Paz

Budworm
and borate

This page and overleaf Hawkins and Power's rare Liberator parked on the ramp at Chandler Airfield, Arizona, in February 1984. 'Bomb doors' agape, this converted B-24 can haul 2000 US gal (18,250 lb) of fire-retardant borate.

47

A spraying specialist, Chandler-based Biegert
Aviation own a sizable fleet of C-54s. N44909 is a
particularly handsome example

A good pre-owned C-54 can be bought for under $100,000 from the Aerospace Maintenance and Regeneration Center (formerly MASDC) at Davis Monthan AFB, Arizona. Aero Union Corporation are the experts when it comes to converting old airliners into borate bombers or budworm sprayers to Standard Transport Category standard. A ventral pannier with a borate capacity of 3000 US gal (limited to a 2000 US gal uplift on the C-54 for centre of gravity reasons) is the biggest single modification. N963581/'160' stands ready for the call to haul

C-54 '117' warms its natural metal finish in the
strong Arizona sunshine

Under normal circumstances, Conair would be a somewhat suspicious name for an aircraft operator, but in this case it refers to the airborne protection of Canada's rich coniferous forests. This borate DC-6, C-GIOY/'48' stands illuminated under a rain laden sky

Overleaf Fire is an obvious and spectacular consumer of wood. But there is a more insidious enemy lurking in the depths of the forest. As dawn breaks out over northern Quebec, it's time to start pumping 'goop' into Conifair's spraying fleet for a concerted attack against insect pests such as the spruce budworm, hemlock looper and jackpine sawfly

Constellation C-GXKR is one of a pair of lusty 749ers operated by Conifair Aviation Inc

Right A Conifair Connie in full cry at the start of a spraying run

Goop is a cocktail of diesel fuel and malathion with a dash of red dye to aid visual monitoring. Although it's bad news for budworms, the spray is at worst a passing irritant to other forest creatures. Calm conditions are required for a smooth, accurate application. When the going gets rough, the goop stops flowing

T & G Aviation of Chandler, Arizona, is probably the world's biggest operator of DC-7 borate bombers. DC-7C N5903 looks to be in superb condition

One of Conifair's four DC-4s (C-GXKN), just after a smart re-spray at Saint Jean Airport

Top right In its heyday the DC-7C 'Seven Seas' was a peerless performer. Thanks to its quintessential aerodynamics and abundant power, the 7C could carry over 100 cosseted passengers non-stop across the North Atlantic (the first aircraft to do so) at 345 mph, even against the strength-sapping jetstreams encounted on the westerly route. The 7C was the ultimate development of the magnificent 'Seven', which

was also the first airliner to fly non-stop from coast to coast across the United States, a feat it achieved in November 1953. Douglas dominated the market for four-engined transports, building a total of 2284. Almost 30 years after it rolled off the production line at Santa Monica, N90802 now sports a ventral borate tank with a capacity of 3000 US gal (27,375 lb). **Right** The Wright Stuff: the 7C is powered by four mighty 3400 hp TC18 Turbo-Compound (R-3350-EA1) 18-cylinder two-row radials housed in titanium nacelles. The port inner needs a spinner

Douglas built the last of 121 DC-7Cs in 1958;
Arizona is probably home for most of the handful
which survive

Heads and tails: a DC-6B sticks its nose into a gaggle of C-54s

Water-wings

Grumman is justly renowned for its outstanding contribution to naval aviation, especially the 'cat' family of famous fighters perpetuated by the F-14 Tomcat. The G-21 Goose of 1937 was a rare foray into the civil market which drew on the company's experience with the aquatic J2F Duck biplane. This See Bee Air G-21A retains the original fit of close-coupled 450 hp Pratt & Whitney R-985-SB-2 engines; from 1958 McKinnon Enterprises offered two, four 340 hp Lycoming versions (G-21C/D, the latter with a lengthened bow) and PT6A turboprop conversions (G-21E/G). The neat retractable wing-tip floats are non-standard, almost certainly a McKinnon touch

Wasp R-1340s blaring, a Grumman G-73 Mallard (N1208) begins a scenic trip across the Virgin Islands

After getting its feet wet, the Mallard powers
away in a flurry of spray. Since March 1982,
Virgin Islands Sea Plane Shuttle Inc have operated
the routes relinquished by Antilles Air Boats

Manoeuvring an amphib on the water is a tad difficult even in ideal conditions; in a fickle current, heavy swell or strong crosswind it can be downright infuriating. After a successful splashdown, the pilot of this Antilles Air Boats' Goose guns his starboard engine to bring the bow into line for the run in to the beaching area; good rudder coordination helps him to steer a true course. **Overleaf** Back for another cargo of sun-worshippers

Grumman teamed with Resorts International to produce the G-111, a 28-seat commuter conversion of the HU-16 Albatross. Chalk's operate three G-111s; N116FB heads back to Watson Island in downtown Miami after a flight from Nassau in the Bahamas. The first G-111, N112FB, exhibited at the NBAA convention in Kansas City in 1980, is in the background (right) behind a PT6-powered G-73T Turbo Mallard.
Overleaf Bimini in the Bahamas: a Chalk's Mallard waits for the OK from the customs and immigration office

Prop pot-pourri

Douglas DC-3A EI-AYO is now safely tucked away in the Science Museum's hangar at Wroughton near Swindon after being retrieved from open storage at Shannon, Eire, in October 1978. Originally NC16071, it served with United Air Lines from December 1936 until August 1954, when it was acquired by the Enhart Manufacturing Company of Hartford, Connecticut and re-registered N333H. Interestingly, NC16071 was one of the initial batch of 15 DC-3As delivered to United; all had the cabin door placed on the right to be consistent with the carrier's Boeing 247s. United also specified 1200 hp Pratt & Whitney R-1830-92 Twin Wasp radials to give the DC-3 enough power to fly routes over the Rockies with a fair safety margin

Despite the introduction of new equipment (HS.748s, for example) SATENA's fleet of DC-3s and C-47s continue to perform the vital social service of providing a reliable link between the industrialized areas of Columbia and its underdeveloped rural regions. The port engine of this C-47 (FAC1120) comes under scrutiny during a turnround check

Right The DC-3 celebrated its 50th birthday in December 1985 and the world's most famous transport airplane remains as irreplaceable as ever. N230F pauses for reflection

The legend really began with the DST (Douglas Sleeper Transport), certificated on 21 May 1936. Interestingly, the original DST layout featured a separate berth for honeymoon couples, but the idea was discarded before the airplane entered service. Pity

Taxi Aéreo: DC-3 HK-329 of El Venado pauses between operations at Villavicencio, Columbia, in October 1977

Overleaf Plinth-mounted DC-3 CF-CPY in Canadian Pacific livery is the star attraction at Whitehorse Airport in the Yukon Territory

Opposite page SATENA DC-4 FAC691 on the ramp at Bogota in May 1984 before departing on a flight to Puerto Asis in southern Columbia via Neiva and Florencia. **This page** En route: the flight-deck of FAC691 is the vantage point as the Andes rise into view before being partially screened by a layer of cloud. Mountains and forced landings don't mix

SATENA (*Servicio Aeronavegación a Territorios Nacionales*) is operated by the Colombian Air Force at the behest of the government to provide a lifeline for small, remote communities—a commercially untenable task for unsubsidized private airlines. **Above** SATENA's two DC-4s, FAC691 and FAC695, ready for inspection; meticulous maintenance keeps 'em flying. **Right** North American influence permeates the design of the uniforms worn by SATENA personnel, but their professionalism is homegrown

Roughly 20 DC-4s remain in airline service and the majority fly in South American skies. The strut under the tail of FAC695 prevents the aircraft tipping over during loading operations, when the centre of gravity can easily exceed the aft limit. Before takeoff the load will have been properly distributed to put the CG where it should be, forward of the main gears

Until 1980, Eldorado Aviation employed a couple
of DC-4s to supply cargo and company employees
to uranium mines in Saskatchewan and other
locations on northern Canada. This example is
being loaded at Edmonton before making a night-
time departure to Uranium City

Rescued from the boneyard at Tucson, Arizona, this C-54 has been restored to pristine condition. The assorted junk in the background won't be so lucky

DC-4 N67029 stripped back to bear metal during restoration work at San Jose, California, in September 1983. **Overleaf** DC-6B N2296B still manages to look majestic despite being parked amid the aeronautical trash at Tucson in February 1984. This airplane is also featured on the front cover

Super Constellation N73544 at Camarillo Airport near Burbank in January 1984 after an eventful ferry flight from Chino, a journey punctuated by an engine shutdown and numerous expletives from her crew. LA-based Classic Air purchased this ex-US Air Force C-121C after the Connie became surplus to spraying requirements. A stillborn attempt to refurbish the airplane for passenger services, which included a half-hearted attack with a spray gun, seems to have ended in stalemate

After a patient three-year wait by its ace reporter and photographer, *Propliner* scooped every other aviation magazine in the world when it carried a major feature on the Super Constellations operated by the Indian Air Force and Navy. Pictured at Lohegaon AFB, Pune, on 6 January 1984, BG583 (foreground) made its last flight in November 1983; the airplane is currently held in storage pending a decision to fly her to the Air Force museum in New Delhi. Like the other eight Indian Connies, this 1049G was a hand-me-down from flag carrier Air India

BG579 began her Air Force career in 1962 and served continuously with No 6 Sqn, transporting personnel and general cargo throughout the Indian subcontinent until she was withdrawn from service on 31 March 1984. During the course of his on-the-spot report, Stephen Piercey made a 28-minute flight aboard this aircraft from Pune to Santa Cruz—the highlight of an historic visit

Left Despite some corrosion problems in the belly area (the toilets were put off-limits to contain it), the serviceable Air Force Connies were still in outstanding condition

The Indian Navy assumed responsibility for all maritime patrol duties in 1976, and five 1049s were duly transferred from the Air Force inventory to equip No 312 Sqn. All the aircraft were modified for their new role and featured a Thorn EMI ASV.21 multi-mode search radar mounted in a ventral 'dustbin' behind the nosewheel doors. IN317 still wore Air Force uniform when she made her last flight in December 1983; the aircraft is currently in open storage at Goa

IN316 has never been the same since the landing gear was retracted accidentally as it taxied at Goa on 11 January 1983. Fortunately, the Indian Navy received a batch of Soviet Ilyushin Il-38s to replace the clapped-out Connies

Down and out

DC-7B N90770 will remain stranded at Tucson, despite the characteristically jaunty angle adopted by the nosewheel. With no engines, the cutting torch provides the only way out

DC-7B N4889C still has her full complement of Turbo Compounds, but who needs a thirsty 'Seven' without a strengthened cargo floor? Incidentally, the extended wing centre section added to the 7C lengthened the span by 10 ft (to 127 ft 6 in) and pushed the engines further outboard, a feature which reduced drag and set a new low in cabin noise and vibration

Wings clipped forever, a C-46 waits for the *coup de grâce* at La Paz behind an intact CAMBA Martin 4-0-4, CP-1570

Top and right Once the sexiest shape on the ramp, this DC-4 now brightens the backlot at La Paz. **Above** If this DC-6 ever flies again, it will become the world's largest glider

Almost certainly the only surviving Boeing 377 Stratocruiser, N74603 resides at Tucson International Airport. Bought by Aero Spacelines of Van Nuys, California, as a source of spares for its famous Guppy conversion programme, the Strat remained largely intact until it became a repository for aircraft parts after the tail was removed in 1982. Boeing only built a limited edition of 50 'Statuscruisers' and N74603 was one of a batch of ten delivered to Northwest Airlines

Powered by four 3500 hp Pratt & Whitney
R-4360 Wasp Majors, the big Boeing had a
cruising speed of 325 mph and transatlantic range.
Pictured in January 1984, the sun had yet to erase
her original Northwest livery; the *Stratocruiser*
script is still visible below the flight-deck windows

Overleaf A grounded DC-6 at La Paz with only
50 per cent power remaining; the engines have
probably been retained as ballast

A forlorn C-121A Super Constellation (ex-0-80610) skulks in the twilight zone at Davis Monthan AFB in Arizona. Named *The Columbine*, this special 749 was used by five-star General Dwight D. Eisenhower in 1950–51 during his term as Supreme Commander Allied Forces in Europe

This page and overleaf It shouldn't happen to a lady: the same airplane rotting away in an ocean of unwanted aluminium

The final perch of a rare bird: a VC-121C struggles to maintain its sense of balance and an aura of dignity

Above A derelict Indian Air Force Super Constellation out to grass at Pune

Overleaf A motley line-up of decrepit C-54 Skymasters

A C-118 Liftmaster (ex-0-33245) takes root

With a Constellation for company this C-54 will
keep its parking space for a good while yet

If you're in the market for a C-118, mosey-on-down to Bobs' Airpark

Right Glory daze: two DC-7Cs stare into oblivion

Overleaf For Steve (Wright R-3350, Super Constellation 1049, HI-207)